Sila and the Land

Sila and the Land was made possible through Climate Action 150, an initiative focused on leveraging youth-led inquiry, action and voice in order to create a climate resilient and just Canada for the next 150 years. Managed by GreenLearning Canada, the project involved collaboration with a range of partners including TakingITGlobal who provided an opportunity for Indigenous youth leaders to share their perspectives on climate change through this book.

This project was undertaken with the financial support of the Catherine Donnelly Foundation and the Government of Canada through the federal department of Environment and Climate Change.

Connected North

This project was undertaken with the financial support of:
Ce projet a été réalisé avec l'appui financier de:

Environnement et Changement climatique Canada

Environment and Climate Change Canada

A portion of the proceeds of the book will go toward the Native Youth Sexual Health Network and their work bringing attention to the impacts of environmental violence on Indigenous health, rights and justice.

The process behind *Sila and the Land* is an important part of the story. Three young Indigenous women came together to write a children's book that could help share perspectives on the land common across First Nations, Métis and Inuit communities. This includes a shared respect for the earth and an understanding of our responsibilities to protect it for future generations.

In order to convey these perspectives in the story, the authors spoke with youth from a number of Indigenous communities across Canada. They asked about why the environment was important to each of them and what land based teachings and experiences were significant to their identities and cultures. Their responses helped shape the book, offering examples of things Sila could learn from the land during her journey travelling across the North, East, South and West.

It is important to note that while there are shared perspectives across Indigenous communities there are also many differences. This book does not claim to represent any specific cultures or teachings, but instead encourages children and youth to seek out knowledge from the territories that they are living on. It also aims to inspire other young Indigenous writers and illustrators to believe in their gifts and the power of their stories.

Sila lived with her Grandmother in a cozy, little house that kept them warm during harsh Arctic winters. On one sunny day, the birds were singing and all you could hear were the sounds of nature. Sila came home from school and ran straight to her Grandmother to tell her all about her day.

“Grandmother! Today we learned about the environment and how every culture has a relationship to the land!”

Grandmother smiled and replied, “That’s wonderful Sila!”

They gave each other a hug and walked over to the window.

“What is our culture’s relationship to the land?” Sila asked.

“Well, it is within you of course! It is in your blood.”

“How can I learn more about our culture though? Are there any books I can read?”

Then Grandmother explained “You can find all the answers outside by interacting with the environment around you. Although it is important to learn through books, it is also important to engage yourself with your community and with the land – that way you also learn more about yourself. Now, why don’t you go for a walk and explore your surroundings. The land is where you will find all the answers to anything in life if only you search hard enough.”

“Yes Grandmother, but which direction should I go?” asked Sila.

“Follow your instincts and let them guide you.”

As Sila walked out the front door of her house, right away she noticed the wondrous beauty of her environment, something that she did not notice before. She loved the sight of the flowers so much that she wanted to pick as many as she could. There were dozens of purple saxifrages surrounding her house and a little ways away, the ground was covered with crowberries.

She said to herself, "I would love to wake up to these wonderful flowers in my room! And these crowberries would go great with the bannock Grandmother makes!"

A caribou heard Sila's excitement and so he decided to walk up and greet her.

"Hello child," said the caribou.

Sila greeted him back, "Good afternoon."

Then the caribou asked, "Do you really like these flowers and berries?"

She smiled a big smile, "Oh yes, I would really like to keep as many of these as I can!"

The caribou was amused by her excitement, "If you really respected the flowers and berries, it would be best to let them grow. If you pick them all you would be killing them and not leaving any for others."

Sila frowned at this, but let the caribou continue, "If you think they are a pretty sight, do not worry; they will be here again tomorrow for you to admire. You should always be sure to only take what you need and remember what your ancestors and grandparents have taught you. Just like how you need to be respectful of the flowers and berries, the same goes for animals. When you have killed a caribou like me in order to feed your family, you must remember to be grateful for my selflessness. It is also important to use every part of the carcass, so as not to waste."

Sila took what the caribou said very seriously and thought about the amount of crowberries she had picked. She realized that she had too many, so she offered the caribou some of her portion. She then left the flowers alone to grow and went off on her way after thanking the caribou for his wisdom.

Sila kept thinking about what the caribou had said to her about why it is so important to be grateful for the plants and animals.

She walked for a few minutes and then her thoughts came to a stop as she came across a ptarmigan perched on top of a boulder. Sila always admired birds because of their ability to fly. She said hello and the ptarmigan greeted her back, "Hi, child."

The ptarmigan could see how deep in thought Sila was so she asked, "What is the matter little one?"

Sila told the ptarmigan what was on her mind, "I came across a caribou who taught me the importance of preserving animals and plants, and now I am wondering what would happen if all the plants were to disappear."

The ptarmigan then said, "Little one, your people have a principle for just that. It is the idea of taking the long view which means looking at things ahead of us and ahead of time".

"How can I take the long view?" Sila asked.

The ptarmigan explained, "Think of the importance of the plants around you. Ask yourself, what do you need them for?"

Sila thought hard and smiled. She remembered what her grandmother had taught her during an afternoon walk they had gone on before. She shared with the ptarmigan, "Plants can be used for many things! Like, medicines, teas, and food for us and the animals."

"Very good, that is right. Now keeping that in mind, think about what it would be like if the plants were no longer there," the ptarmigan said.

Sila thought hard once more, "Well, we would not be able to make our medicines out of plants, so we would not have anything to make us feel better. Also, some animals only eat plants and they would no longer have anything to eat. If the animals are gone, we would not be able to eat them either."

"Exactly. As a ptarmigan, I am able to fly high and look upon miles and miles of land. I am aware of what is yet to come. But, since humans cannot fly you must find other ways to take the long view. You can do this by thinking about your actions because every choice has a consequence."

Before the ptarmigan flew away, Sila thanked it and then continued or her journey.

Walking East, Sila decided to take a little rest and sat on a large rock. The rock sensed the magnitude of history Sila had within her and her strength to carry it everywhere she goes.

"Young child, I sense a long line of history within you, given by your ancestors. You must honor it by making sure to carry it with pride wherever you go."

Sila heard these words, but could not tell where they were coming from. It sounded like it was deep and rumbling around her. It seemed so strong and wise, it almost frightened her.

The rock sensed her fear and reassured her not to be afraid,

"Do not worry, young one, it is I the rock, as you call me, speaking to you."

Then Sila asked, "Why is it important to carry my history with me?"

"As a rock, I have lived for millions of years, and throughout those long years I have had the strength of carrying knowledge with me from many people and their ancestors. I carry knowledge that others may not see as well like the history of the animals, plants, and the shaping of the land."

Sila was curious as to how old the rock may be, "How long have you been around for?"

The rock answered, "It is not just how long I have been around that is significant, it is how much knowledge and experience I have gathered and carried that is important. That is what makes up who I am, just like you. You have the knowledge and history of your ancestors to carry as well as the knowledge you will learn throughout your short life. This knowledge is what you need to pass down to future generations in order to strengthen your culture."

From the rock's encouraging words, Sila felt ready to continue on her journey once more. She thanked the rock and went on her way.

Suddenly, Sila realized how thirsty her adventure had made her. Out in the distance she saw a glimmering river and started walking towards it. When she got there, she kneeled and cupped a handful of water to her mouth.

A salmon noticed Sila and swam up because he was curious as to what could make such a little girl so thirsty, "Why are you so thirsty little one?"

Sila then replied, "I have journeyed from the North in order to gain knowledge about my culture and our relationship to the land. I have already learned so much."

"Ah, you are exploring. You know fish like me are great at exploring," the salmon said.

"Is that so?" Sila asked.

"Yes, us fish must travel far distances in the waters until we mature. But, we never forget to go back to where we came from; we always remember where home is."

"What do you do then once you return home?" asked Sila.

"We share the experience we gained with others. We share the knowledge we have gained with each other so that others will learn as well. So, do not forget to return home and to reflect on your journey, as well as on what you experienced and share what you learned with the people around you. Will you do that for me, little one?"

Sila thought of how proud Grandmother will be when she tells her the story of her adventure. She smiled at the salmon and agreed, "Of course I will remember to share my knowledge."

After drinking some more water, Sila decided to turn South and wondered what she would find this time. Sila noticed how different her surroundings were now from when she started up North, but she felt comfortable as if she were at home no matter what part of the land she was in.

Sila walked through the forest, looking at all the plants and critters running back and forth across the dirt path. As she wandered through, she came across a maple tree that stood tall and strong above the other trees.

The maple tree spoke to Sila in a soft voice, "What brings you to such an old tree like me, little one?"

Sila looked up and answered, "I was just wandering around thinking… wait, why can't I see you?"

"I am the great maple tree and need no face to speak, no mouth to eat, no eyes to see, and no ears to listen. When you speak I can understand you by the way you feel, your roots speak to me."

"My roots? I don't have any roots. I'm a person, not a tree!" Sila said.

"Oh, but you do have roots, little one. Your roots are what connect you to your ancestors of your home. Your roots are what keep you strong and allow you to stand tall. With your roots, you can hold on tight to your family, culture and the land you wander now. You came from the land, little one, so you have roots just as I do that are in your blood and traditions. You may not see yours as you see mine, but they are there and just as deep."

Sila sat quietly and thought about her Grandmother; about her language and teachings she has learned. "Why haven't you been knocked down though? You're old."

The deep laugh of the tree sent the leaves shaking. The maple answered, "I may be old, but my work on this earth is not done, just as yours is just beginning. Walk now, little human, enjoy my forest and see who else speaks to you. Listen, not just with your ears, but with your roots as well."

Sila said nothing as she thought about what the maple had to say, listening not with only her eyes but with her roots too. After a couple of moments, she started walking and looked back once more to see the maple dancing in the wind. She waved to the tree and then continued her journey forward.

The wind blew Sila's hair around her face as she walked and she felt like it was carrying her off her feet!

"Stop that!" She yelled.

"Who wishes for me to stop?" A deep voice spoke from behind her, but no one was there.

"I do. You almost took me away!" Sila raised her voice over the roaring wind around her.

"Well then, I am sorry, but I have a message for you to hear," He said.

"Who are you?"

"Why, I am the one who pushes the clouds of rain to water the land below, who dries the flooded earth and who pushes the boats along the water to new lands. I am the wind and the air."

"Well you almost knocked me down and then tried to take me away!" Sila exclaimed.

"But you didn't get taken away; as the great maple told you, your roots run deep just as his do and because of this I could not take you." They walked together along the path and he continued, "When you are the wind you show force in everything you do. You can become like a storm and push away those that try to hurt you and you push until there is nothing left in your path and you may walk once more. Always stand up for what is right; never back down and keep a clear mind as you push through any challenges that get in your way."

"But I am so small. How can I do that?"

"You will not be small forever, little one. You will grow stronger and stronger and as you do, always remember us and the things we have taught you. Remember the gentle caribou, the wise ptarmigan, the ancient rock, the loyal salmon, the sturdy maple tree and of course me, the wind. Remember all of the land and we will help you push through your most difficult times."

Sila looked around and suddenly things became very still.

Up in the sky, Sila could see an eagle flying high above. His cry was loud and fierce as he circled her and then came swooping down. His wings were so powerful the gust of air caused Sila to fall down.

"You knocked me down you know, that wasn't very nice!" Sila frowned and crossed her arms.

"I am sorry, please forgive me little Sila, I am the eagle. I soar the skies and watch over everyone down below."

"I forgive you, but how do you know my name?" she asked.

"We all know your name Sila. You are a very important little girl you know."

"Oh yeah, why is that?"

"Because you will be the one to change the world. You will be the one to see."

"But can't we all see?"

"Sadly, not all of us can. Hop on my back and I shall show you what many refuse to see."

As they flew through the air heading West, the eagle directed Sila to look at the water.

She looked down and saw that the water was not the clean and clear colour she knew, it was cloudy and dirty.

“What is wrong with the water? Why can I not see the fish beneath the surface or any plants growing near it? Where is all that garbage coming from and why is there black oil covering the top and all over those animals?”

Sila started feeling very sad seeing how sick the water and the land were below.

"The world is sick Sila and can't get better without the help of you and other people. Humans are damaging the earth and water in many ways and causing something called climate change. This change is taking many forms and causing lots of problems all over the world." The eagle dipped a talon into the water and dragged it as they flew.

"Look behind us and what do you see?"

"I see the ripples growing bigger and bigger," she said.

"Exactly, our actions always have consequences. Just as the water ripples out and affects other things, so do our actions on the earth. You must learn to be careful with what you do and not think only of the impacts on tomorrow, but think of years from now. Think of the children that will come after you and the ones that will come after them. If we let the water, the land, the plants and the animals keep becoming more sick they won't be here for future generations."

The eagle continued, "The water is especially important for us to take care of because it is one of the most sacred medicines we have on this earth."

"Because we need it to live?" Sila asked.

"Yes. It heals us. It heals our minds when we can no longer think clearly. It heals our body when we can no longer stand on our own. It heals our soul when we feel lost and alone. Our water heals us because our mother earth loves us, but we must give back by protecting it from pollution and climate change."

The eagle landed beside the dirty water and let Sila take a closer look.

"But I am so young and don't yet have enough knowledge. I can't save the world and all of the water."

"You will, little Sila. You will keep learning and people will help you, do not turn them away. Be kind and open with them for you are all the future of this earth.You must first start with yourself and then connect what you know with the wisdom and support of others. No matter where you are on the land we are all connected and need to work together."

The eagle flew back North, back over the water and soon they were in front of Sila's home. Sila climbed off of the eagle and stood in front of her house.

"Remember Sila, you can change the world."

"Will I see you again?" Sila became sad as the eagle started to fly away.

"Of course you will. You will hear my cries in the wind and know that I am watching over you, but for now go back to your Grandmother. Share what you have learned today with her and other people in your community and around the world. Share with the world about how much our earth teaches us, but also how much it is hurting. Start making change for a better world; for you and the generations coming after you."

Sila waved goodbye and went back into her cozy home where Grandmother was sitting waiting for her. She started telling her all about the fantastic journey she had across all four directions of the land. She talked about the animals and plants she had met as well as the things she learned and what she should do to help them. The day of exploring and learning had made Sila quite tired though and so she crawled into bed.

With a proud look in her eyes, Grandmother leaned over and gave her a gentle kiss goodnight.

"A perfect ending to a perfect day,"
she said with a smile.

"No Grandmother, not an ending, a beginning. A beginning to something wonderful."

Take Action

Protecting the land for future generations is all of our responsibilities. Here are a few ways that children and adults can get involved.

- **Keep Learning.** Seek out knowledge that will help build your understanding of the causes and impacts of climate change. Be critical of where you are getting information from and be sure to learn from Indigenous perspectives. There are many resources out there including books, articles, art, documentaries, web videos and people that can help guide you.
- **Change Your Habits.** Think about the things you do each day and how these actions impact the environment. Look for ways that you can conserve energy, use less water, reduce waste and create less pollution.
- **Hold People in Power Accountable.** Sometimes politicians and leaders of companies need encouragement to do what is best for the environment. Stay informed about what decisions are being made and let them know that fighting climate change is important to you.
- **Start Your Own Initiative.** Think about starting a special club, project, campaign or organization of your own dedicated to protecting the land and wildlife. Involve people who also care about these issues and work together to raise awareness and push for change.
- **Support Indigenous Rights Movements.** Respecting the land and taking care of it for future generations is a big part of Indigenous cultures around the world. Traditional knowledge and practices have been passed on through thousands of years of living on the land and so by protecting the rights of Indigenous peoples you can help share this knowledge and restore balance.
- **Reflect, Connect and Give Thanks.** Take time each day to honour your personal relationship to the land. Get outside and take in your surroundings; notice the beauty of the land, water, air, and animals and how they are all connected. Be open to what the land can teach you and show gratitude for all that it offers.

Resources

VICELAND's 'Rise' Video Series
Video series capturing resistance and protection of land across Indigenous communities in the Americas.
www.viceland.com/en_us/show/rise

CBC's '8th Fire' Media Collection
A collection of documentaries, book lists, maps and other resources uncovering the history of conflict, colonialism and denial since the arrival of Europeans on the land now called Canada.
www.cbc.ca/8thfire

Indigenous Environmental Network
An alliance of Indigenous Peoples whose shared mission is to protect the sacredness of Mother Earth from contamination and exploitation by respecting and adhering to Indigenous knowledge and natural law.
www.ienearth.org

Indigenous Climate Action
An Indigenous-led initiative focused on filling the gaps between lived experiences of Indigenous Peoples and the policies and strategies being developed to address climate change.
www.indigenousclimateaction.com

GoodMinds.com
Online bookstore with First Nations, Métis and Inuit resources for all age levels.
www.goodminds.com

Inhabit Media
Inuit owned publishing company focused on stories that preserve Inuit culture and language.
www.inhabitmedia.com

TakingITGlobal's Commit2Act and Action Guides
A free tracking tool with tips for climate change prevention and frameworks for planning your own initiative.
www.commit2act.org | *www.tigweb.org/guide*

Become a Changemaker
A collection of resources to help youth develop the skills to become empowered to change the world for the better.
www.helptakeaction.com

Red Rising Magazine
An Indigenous magazine focused on celebrating Indigenous resistance, resilience and creativity through stories and art.
www.redrisingmagazine.ca

The Nunavut Climate Change Centre
A web-based climate change resource centre intended to provide current climate change information relevant to the people of Nunavut.
www. climatechangenunavut.ca

Whose Land
A project bringing together land acknowledgements from across the country and an interactive map highlighting the traditional territories, treaties, and Indigenous communities across Canada.
www.whose.land

We Matter
An Indigenous-led non-profit committed to Indigenous youth empowerment, hope and life promotion.
www.wemattercampaign.org

About the Authors

Shelby Angalik is from Arviat Nunavut, an Inuit hamlet on the western shore of Hudson Bay. Her strong voice and courageous spirit has led her to a number of leadership opportunities where she has shared perspectives on topics such as literacy, climate change and the importance of Inuit traditional knowledge. Shelby cares deeply about empowering Indigenous youth to draw strength from their traditional values and to return to their languages as tools for understanding and protecting the land.

Ariana Roundpoint is wolf clan of the Kanien'kehakah people, born and raised in Akwesasne. She has a strong passion for culture revitalization, important work that is needed in order to protect Indigenous knowledge and ways of life for the upcoming generations. A central part of this work for Ariana is to increase awareness of how traditions are being lost and the harm that is being done to Mother Earth. She has a lot planned for her future and wishes to influence others to create change by spreading knowledge through her writing.

Lindsay DuPré is a Métis social worker and educator. She was born in Mississauga and has lived in Southern Ontario for most of her life, but attributes much of her knowledge and growth to the land and people from many different Indigenous nations. Lindsay focuses her gifts on areas such as Indigenous education, youth leadership, mental health and life promotion leveraging the power of stories to heal and shift perspectives. Lindsay is committed to helping mobilize the growing network of First Nations, Métis and Inuit youth fighting for social and environmental justice.

About the Illustrator

Halie Finney was born and raised in the Lesser Slave Lake region of Alberta where generations of her family have also called home. As an artist, Halie investigates her Métis heritage and how family deals with inevitable change in a place where things seem to remain the same. Currently, Halie resides in Edmonton, Alberta where she continues to work on her art practice.

Manufactured by Amazon.ca
Acheson, AB